Christmas Programs

FOR THE CHURCH

Plays, poems, and ideas
for a meaningful celebration!

Compiled by
Elaina Meyers

Standard®
PUBLISHING
Bringing The Word to Life

www.standardpub.com

Scripture taken from the *HOLY BIBLE, NEW INTERNATIONAL VERSION*®. *NIV*®. Copyright © 1973, 1978, 1984 by Biblica, Inc.™ Used by permission of Zondervan. All rights reserved.

Editorial team: Elaina Meyers, Courtney Rice
Cover design: Brigid Naglich
Inside design: Bob Korth

Published by Standard Publishing
Cincinnati, Ohio
www.standardpub.com
Copyright © 2010 by Standard Publishing
All rights reserved.

ISBN 9780-7847-2355-5

Contents

DRAMAS & SKITS

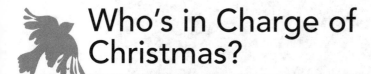

Who's in Charge of Christmas?

DIANNE McINTOSH

Summary: POLLY, a take-charge church volunteer, must hand over some of her responsibilities at Christmas time in order to see who's really in charge of Christmas.

Characters:
POLLY—feisty, out-spoken woman
EDITH—level-headed woman
Props: tissue
Setting: church foyer
Running Time: 8 minutes

POLLY and EDITH are standing center stage.

POLLY: Edith, I don't understand what's going on at this church.

EDITH: What don't you understand?

POLLY: Well, last year *Bernice* was in charge of the Giving Baskets.

EDITH: Polly, Bernice died.

POLLY: *[takes a deep breath]* Edith, I know she died. That's beside the point. The point is *I* should be in charge now. *I* was second in command. For ten years *I* was her right-hand woman.

EDITH: But Polly you're already so busy. You organize the Christmas dinner, you decorate the sanctuary for Christmas, you iron those little white dollies for the communion table, you choose flowers all year long, and . . .

POLLY: Oh be quiet Edith, you're making me tired. I know I have some minor duties around the church but I want to be in charge of those Giving Baskets! I was next in line to take them over.

EDITH: Polly, what's so important about being in charge of the Giving Baskets?

POLLY: *[gasp]* How can you ask that?

EDITH: Because I haven't the faintest idea why you, the busiest woman at this church, would want to be in charge of yet another project.

POLLY: Think about it Edith. Where's the focus at Christmas time?

EDITH: Jesus?

POLLY: *[condescendingly]* Besides Jesus, think Edith, it's those Giving Baskets. And what do people think of when they think of "Giving Baskets?"

EDITH: *[hesitantly]* Giving?

POLLY: Edith, Edith, Edith . . . please don't over simplify everything. *[triumphantly]* They think "Bernice."

EDITH: *[incredulously]* Really?

POLLY: Of course they do. Everyone thinks how wonderful she is, how *giving* she is, how . . . well . . . how "Mrs. Christmas" she is. Now she's gone and it's *[taps on chest with fingers]* my turn to be Mrs. Christmas, *[emphatically uses both hands to tap on chest]* it's my turn Edith *[pause]* but what happens?

EDITH: Sally Virtroth is asked to take care of the Giving Baskets.

POLLY: Exactly. And to make matters worse, they had the audacity to ask *me* to help her.

EDITH: You've been robbed.

POLLY: *[dabs at eyes with a tissue]* Yes, *[sniffs]* robbed. By this time next month everyone will think of Sally Virtroth as "Mrs. Christmas" and I'll just be the dollie ironer, the worker woman, the behind the scenes helper person. It's a tragedy.

EDITH: *[shakes her head]* POLLY! Listen to yourself. You'd think you wanted to be the savior of the world.

POLLY: Well . . . not the world . . . but . . .

EDITH: *[shakes POLLY's shoulders]* Polly, come on. You have got to be kidding! Jesus is Christmas. *[emphasis on every word]* He has to be the only focus. The

Who's in Charge of Christmas?

Giving Baskets are simply an expression of *His* love—that's it. I can't believe you've been waiting around to be "Mrs. Christmas."

POLLY: Well, I didn't exactly say that. I just . . .

EDITH: Listen Polly, you can try to be in charge all you want, but that won't change who's *really* in charge.

POLLY: No?

EDITH: No! Jesus, *[emphatically]* "Mr. Christmas," is in charge. Remember, the baby in the manger grows up and dies on the cross for the sins of the world and then, on the third day, rises from the grave?

POLLY: Edith, I fully comprehend the role of Jesus in Christmas. *[looks off into the distance and builds volume with each declaration]* I know His significance as the Son of God, Wonderful, Counselor, Bright and Morning Star, the . . .

EDITH: The guy in charge of the Giving Baskets?

POLLY: *[deflated]* . . . in charge of the *[pause]* Giving Baskets? *[shakes head, sighs]* You're right Edith; He's even in charge of the Giving Baskets.

[POLLY and EDITH are silent for a moment. EDITH takes a deep breath and looks sheepishly at POLLY.]

EDITH: Yes . . . and with that thought in mind . . . *[stops, takes a deep breath, then talks quickly]* I was asked to tell you that Twila Tenbetter is going to be in charge of decorating the sanctuary for Christmas this year.

POLLY: *[yells]* What?! I've decorated that sanctuary for the last twenty years!

EDITH: Exactly. So someone new is going to try it this year. Just think of the bright side.

[POLLY looks stunned.]

POLLY: *[dazedly]* What's that?

EDITH: *[cheerfully]* It will give you more time to focus this year.

POLLY: Focus on what?

EDITH: On Jesus, Polly. Simply Jesus.

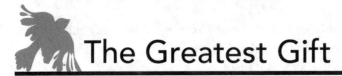

The Greatest Gift

SARAH STASIK

Summary: TOM and RANDY have a contest to see who receives the best gift for Christmas. They reluctantly invite MICHAEL to join the contest, even though they think he is too poor to compete with them. The boys talk ANNA into judging. By the time the judging is over, TOM, RANDY, and ANNA have all learned something from MICHAEL about the greatest gift of all.

Characters:

TOM—rich boy, well dressed

RANDY—rich boy, well dressed

ANNA—friend of boys

MICHAEL—poor boy, dressed in obvious hand-me downs

CAROLERS—small group of singers

Biblical Characters:

ANGEL	SHEPHERD 2
MARY	HEROD
JOSEPH	WISE MAN 1
INN KEEPER	WISE MAN 2
SHEPHERD 1	WISE MAN 3

Setting: Left side of stage setting is modern street corner. Right side of stage is biblical setting that can be used for various scenes.

Props: wrapped bundle to look like baby, three gifts for wise men, staff for shepherd, appropriate costumes for biblical characters

Running Time: 20–30 minutes

SCENE 1:

Tom, Randy, and Anna are talking on a street corner. Michael stands nearby.

TOM: So, what do you think you're getting for Christmas?

RANDY: I bet I get something awesome!

TOM: Yeah, I bet I get everything on my list, and it was a long list. In fact, I bet my stuff is better than yours.

RANDY: No way. I bet I get something that blows all your stuff away. My dad practically came right out and said that I'm getting a Play Station 3.

Tom: Yeah, I asked for that too. But my mom already hinted that I'm getting a big screen TV for my room!

Randy: We should come back here the day after Christmas and see who got the best gift.

Tom: Like a contest?

Randy: Yeah, a contest. Anna can be the judge. Anna, will you?

Anna: Sure.

Tom: What about you? *[looking at Michael]* Wanna be in the contest?

Randy: *[coughs]* I dunno. He couldn't possibly be getting something that will compete with our gifts. It seems kind of mean to ask him.

Anna: It does seem unfair. Everyone knows Michael's parents aren't going to be able to get him something really expensive.

Michael: No, it's okay. I'll be in the contest.

Randy: You sure?

Michael: Yeah, I'm sure.

Tom: Okay, it's settled. The day after Christmas?

Anna, Michael, and **Randy:** Yes, the day after Christmas.

[Anna, Michael, Randy, and Tom exit stage. Carolers enter on street corner and sing a Christmas song.]

SCENE 2:

Carolers exit. Anna, Michael, Randy, and Tom enter on left. On right, Mary enters and sits. Lights are only on four children.

Anna: Time for the contest results! Each of you has to tell me the best gift you received this year, and then I'll pick the winner.

Tom: I'll go first! I got the Play Station 3 with all the accessories and ten games! You guys can come over and play it once I win this contest!

Randy: Whoa, hold on! You aren't going to win this contest, because my gift is so much better than yours! I got the TV mom hinted at and a Nintendo Wii! So, you guys can come over to my house when *I* win the contest!

Tom: So, Anna? Who wins?

Michael: *[clears throat]*

Anna: Umm. We still need to hear about Michael's gift.

Tom: *[looks skeptical]* Oh . . . oh yeah. Okay, Michael, what's the greatest gift you got?

MICHAEL: *[smiling]* The gift I received is the greatest gift ever, because it's a gift that I receive every single day, and will receive every single day for the rest of my life!

RANDY: *[looks more skeptical than TOM]* Really? How'd your parents afford that?

MICHAEL: My parents didn't give me the gift.

TOM: Oh? So, what, do you know a king or something?

MICHAEL: Yes! That's right. Except, not just any king. He is the King of kings!

RANDY: *[crosses arms and looks at Anna]* Okay, Anna, go ahead and pick the winner. And remember, the gifts actually have to be real.

ANNA: We haven't even heard what the gift is yet, Randy. We should at least let him finish.

MICHAEL: I'll have to tell you a story about the king to tell you about the gift.

RANDY/TOM: *[groan/roll eyes]*

ANNA: That sounds fair enough *[louder to RANDY/TOM]* and I'm the judge. So, listen to his story, will you? Go on, Michael.

MICHAEL: Well, the story starts with a young woman named Mary who was visited by an angel.

[Lights dim on four children and move to MARY. MARY is busy with some chore. ANGEL approaches, MARY is startled.]

ANGEL: Do not be afraid! The Lord is with you! You will have a son and name Him Jesus. He will be the Son of God and His Kingdom will go on forever.

MARY: How can this be?

ANGEL: The Holy Spirit will come upon you and you will bear the child who will be called the Son of God. Nothing is impossible with God.

MARY: I am the Lord's servant. May it be as you have said.

[ANGEL exits and lights dim on MARY and move to children. On the dark side of stage, JOSEPH and INN KEEPER join MARY.]

RANDY: Wait, are you telling me an angel shows up, tells Mary she's going to have a baby, and all she says is "let it be as you say"?

MICHAEL: Mary believed in the Lord, and she believed that He could and would do what He said. Remember, the angel told her "nothing is impossible with God," and it's true!

TOM: Well, this story sounds pretty impossible so far.

ANNA: I want to hear more. Let him finish. What will it hurt either of you?

TOM: *[waves Michael ahead]* Go on, then. But hurry up and get to the part about the king.

Michael: Mary and Joseph had to travel to Bethlehem to register for a census that was required by the government.

[Lights dim on children and move to Mary, Joseph, and Inn Keeper.]

Mary: Joseph, I'm very tired and it's almost time for the baby to come!
Joseph: Here's the inn, Mary. Let me check with the inn keeper for a room.
Mary: Hurry Joseph!
Joseph: Sir, do you have a room? My wife is about to have a baby.
Inn Keeper: No. We have no rooms.
Mary: *[holding stomach]* Joseph! It's time!
Joseph: Please, have you no room at all?
Inn Keeper: Only the stable out back.
Joseph: We'll take it. Please show us!

[Mary, Joseph, Inn Keeper exit. Carolers enter and sing Away in a Manger (verse 1). Carolers exit, lights dim and move back to children. Angel and Shepherds enter on dark part of stage.]

Randy: Inns? Stables? No hospitals or doctors? When does this story take place?
Michael: Over two-thousand years ago.
Tom: Oh, man! Michael, are you wasting our time telling us a story about some dead king?
Michael: No! He's still alive!
Anna: After two-thousand years? That's a story we have to hear the end of!
Randy: I guess a two-thousand year old king is pretty cool. Like a movie or something. Go on Michael, let's hear the rest of it.
Michael: It's better than any movie, Randy. So, the baby is born in the stable. His name is Jesus and Mary knows that He is the Son of God. There were shepherds watching their sheep out in the fields nearby that night.

[Lights dim on children, move to Angel and Shepherds. Carolers positioned off stage, but near microphone.]

Angel: Do not be afraid! I bring you news of great joy that will be for all the people! Today in the town of David a Savior has been born to you; he is Christ the Lord. You will find the baby wrapped in strips of cloth and laying in a manger.
Carolers: Glory to God in the highest, peace on Earth, good will to men!

[ANGEL exits.]

SHEPHERD 1: Let's go to Bethlehem and see this child.
SHEPHERD 2: Yes, let's go and worship this king the Lord has sent us!

[SHEPHERDS exit. CAROLERS enter and sing O Come All Ye Faithful (verse 1). CAROLERS exit, lights dim and move back to children. HEROD and WISE MEN enter on dark part of stage.]

MICHAEL: The shepherds went to see baby Jesus, and they knew this child was a gift from God to the whole world. They were joyful and told the story to others.
RANDY: Shepherds and a baby born in a barn. This story is interesting and all, but what about the king and the gift that goes on forever?
TOM: Yeah, what about that gift?
ANNA: And what happens to Mary and the baby?
MICHAEL: I'm getting there. Um, where was I? Oh, yeah. So, there was a king named Herod.
RANDY: Aha! Here's the king!
MICHAEL: No! He's not that king. Anyway, Herod heard that there were wise men from the East who were looking for the King of the Jews. They had followed a star all the way from their land. Now, Herod was worried about this, because he was king and didn't want anyone else to be king.

[Lights dim on children and move to HEROD and WISE MEN. RANDY, TOM, ANNA, and MICHAEL exit, MARY and JOSEPH enter on dark side of stage. MARY holds bundle wrapped like baby.]

HEROD: I have heard there is a child to be born in Bethlehem who will be the shepherd and king of all the people. Is this true?
WISE MAN 1: Yes. We have followed a star to bring gifts to this child.
HEROD: You are very wise. Go and find this child. When you do, come back and tell me where He is, so I may go and worship Him as well.

[HEROD exits stage.]

WISE MAN 2: I don't think we should come back to him.
WISE MAN 3: I agree. I don't trust him.
WISE MAN 1: Let us go and find this child and present our gifts. Then we will return to our country a different way and avoid Herod.

The Greatest Gift

[WISE MEN *move toward* MARY. *Lights brighten across entire stage.* CAROLERS *come onto empty side of stage and sing verse 1 and chorus of* We Three Kings *as* WISE MEN *each kneel and present* MARY *with gifts.* MARY *accepts with smile. When song ends,* MARY, JOSEPH, WISE MEN, *and* CAROLERS *exit stage.* MICHAEL, ANNA, RANDY, *and* TOM *enter.*]

RANDY: So that's it? The king turns out to be scared of the baby? What kind of king is that?

MICHAEL: Herod isn't the king I was talking about.

ANNA: Wow Randy! Didn't you listen to the story? Baby Jesus is the King! Everyone went to worship Him, and wise men came from far away to see Him and bring Him gifts!

TOM: And angels told people about Him. He wasn't just any baby. Even I caught that much.

RANDY: Yeah, I guess so. Okay, so Jesus is born in the manger, and He's the King of kings?

MICHAEL: That's right!

RANDY: So what about the gift? You know, the one you have every day?

MICHAEL: Jesus is the Son of God. God sent Jesus, His only Son, to be born and to die for our sins, so that we could be forgiven and have everlasting life. That means you don't have to be rich to get the gift—the shepherds were the first people to hear from the angels and they weren't rich!

ANNA: Wait, Jesus died?

MICHAEL: Yes, but then He rose to live forever. And if you believe in Him and that God sent Him to die for our sins, then you will have eternal life in the Kingdom of Heaven with Him!

ANNA: Wow! You mean God gave His only Son to save you? That really is the greatest gift.

MICHAEL: [shaking head] No, Anna. God gave His only Son to save *all* of us. Me and you and you and you. [points to each as he says you]. That's the greatest gift of all!

RANDY: Wow. That *is* the greatest gift.

TOM: What about Jesus coming back to life? What about that story?

ANNA: I want to hear about that too. But it's really late.

RANDY: How about tomorrow? Will you come and tell us tomorrow?

MICHAEL: Of course! It's the greatest story ever told!

[Children exit. All characters in play enter and sing Joy to the World.]

The Greatest Gift

Christmas Monologue— Mary's Story

LENORA MCWHORTER

It was a day that changed the world forever. Christmas began in the heart of God, He had a plan to live among His people and to provide a deliverer who would free them from bondage. Before the first Christmas there were struggles and hopelessness among my people. Life was going on as usual with expectations for the long promised Messiah. For some there was a patient longing for a deliverer. Others had been waiting so long they had become apathetic about God's promise to send a Messiah. I was a teenager from a poor family who had been taught that Messiah would come and deliver my people from bondage. From childhood I had come to know of God's love for His people. Many described God's love as measureless, boundless, like a bottomless ocean. I could not perceive such love in my childlike mind but I knew it had to be huge.

Then something unusual happened and not only did my world change but the whole world around me changed. I was engaged to be married to Joseph and was bubbling with joy as I anticipated the day of our wedding. Joseph was quite a gentleman; so kind, thoughtful, and gentle. I sensed right way he would be a good family man, one who would work hard and always honor God. I was pleased that my family had made such a good choice and that it was in God's plan for Joseph and me to come together.

Then one day an angel appeared to me and said, "Mary, you have found favor with God. You will bear a child and He will be a unique child." At first I was in disbelief, then shock, then confused. How could that be when Joseph and I were not yet married? But the angel was clear that the child would be conceived by the Holy Spirit. That was more than my mind could grasp but the angel said, "For with God, nothing shall be impossible." The message was specific that I would have a baby boy and I was to name Him Jesus. It was very humbling to think that God would use me for such an honorable task. I praised God for using me and surrendered to Him to bring to pass all that He had planned. I had dreams and goals for my life but to be used of God in this way exceeded my expectations.

After the angel left me I began to wonder how I would explain this unexplainable miracle to Joseph and what he would think. I soon learned that since this was God's well designed plan He had taken care of everything. An angel appeared to Joseph in a dream and announced that God was up to something big and he put Joseph's mind at ease by telling him that God wanted to use him. Joseph, being an upright man, submitted to God and allowed himself to be used by God to carry out His plan. He took me as his wife and took care of me as I carried the Son of God in my womb. How humble I felt to have been chosen to become the mother of Jesus.

Months passed and the time came for taxation. Joseph had to travel to Bethlehem, a journey of about three days, to register. By this time my pregnancy was approaching full term and I was very heavy. Both Joseph and I had many questions but we kept them to ourselves and pondered them in our hearts. After a long, tiresome journey we arrived in Bethlehem, but many had come ahead of us and the inns were filled. The innkeeper noticed I was weary and worn from the journey. But he said, "I am sorry but we are unable to accommodate you, we are completely filled. All inns in the city are filled to capacity." So there was no chance of getting a room anywhere.

At first I didn't know what to think. For a minute fear gripped me. *What will we do?* I wondered. Joseph sensed my uneasiness and saw the look on my face. He caught my hand and said, "Don't worry Mary. God will help us." Through this whole ordeal I had held on to the angel's words, "With God all things are possible." I knew something needed to happen soon and wondered how God would work this out. As I held my stomach the innkeeper noticed and moved swiftly toward us. "Sir," he said to Joseph. "Come with me. I will take you and your wife to the stable where she will be able to rest." We entered and the cattle stood still as in awe as I gave birth to the Son of God.

Joseph paced back and forth among the animals and marveled at how they allowed their feeding trough to become a bed for Jesus. There was a feeling of wonder in that place as the King of kings was born into the world. Dark became light and it seemed as if the world stood still as God became flesh on that special night.

An Unexpected Christmas

SUSAN SUNDWALL

Summary: Everyone in the Collins house is disgusted with the world's view of Christmas. When Christy finds out her best friend shoplifts a gift for her boyfriend, she decides Christmas is for lunatics. Then some unexpected things happen.

Characters:

BLAKE—eleven-year-old boy

MOM—mother of CHRISTY and BLAKE

CHRISTY—seventeen-year-old girl

DAD—father of CHRISTY and BLAKE

ADDISON—friend of CHRISTY, seventeen

CAROLERS

ROB—boyfriend of CHRISTY, eighteen

Setting: Collins living room two days before Christmas

Props: Christmas tree, three chairs, small table, Bible, shopping bag, cell phone for DAD

Costumes: Modern day clothing for all characters. Scarves for CAROLERS. Shepherd costume for BLAKE.

Running time: 20 minutes

MOM enters, lingering at the tree. She picks up the Bible, sits, and begins to read. BLAKE dashes into the room in his shepherd costume.

BLAKE: *[scratches at head]* Mom, this thing is itchy!

MOM: *[looks up]* Come here, let me see. *[removes head covering]* Oh, this fabric is very rough. I'll fix it for you.

BLAKE: Why do I have to be a shepherd again this year anyway?

MOM: Because you look very handsome in that robe!

[Offstage a door slams. CHRISTY enters carrying shopping bag.]

CHRISTY: Christmas is for lunatics!

BLAKE: Uh, oh, somebody cut you off in traffic again?

CHRISTY: No, little shepherd, not this time.

MOM: You look upset, Christy. Did something happen?

CHRISTY: It's no big deal.

BLAKE: You always say that when it *is* a big deal!

MOM: We can talk about it if you'd like. Blake, will you go and see if we have enough mix for hot chocolate?

BLAKE: Oh, sure, kick me out of the room.

MOM: *[sternly]* Blake, please go and check for me.

BLAKE: Okay, I'm going. *[glares at CHRISTY and exits]*

CHRISTY: Mom, it's no big deal—really. I had a hard time with my math test today and traffic was bad coming home.

MOM: Um—the lunatic part—what's that all about?

CHRISTY: It happens every year. People are rude and selfish and . . . it's Christmas! Don't they know that?

MOM: *[glances at Bible]* You know, I'm not sure they do.

CHRISTY: Well, it doesn't seem to make any difference at all what Christmas really means.

MOM: It's been like that for a long time, Christy . . .

BLAKE: *[interrupts calling from offstage]* Mom! Come and see this!

MOM: Now what? Excuse me, I'll be right back. *[exits]*

CHRISTY: *[loudly]* She's such a thief! And at Christmas too. She's just like that . . . that . . . Grinch on TV—only worse! *[stomps offstage]*

MOM: *[enters]* Christy? Boy, something's really bugging her. *[calls out]* Christy?

BLAKE: *[enters without costume]* Forget it, Mom. She's in her "leave me alone" mood. And thanks for fixing my head piece.

MOM: You're welcome. Do you have your lines memorized for the play?

BLAKE: Yeah, I think I can handle it. *[hand to ear]* What's that I hear? It's a baby! His name is Jesus.

MOM: How about your friend, Devin, how's he doing?

BLAKE: I'm not so sure he's my friend.

MOM: Did something happen?

BLAKE: It sure did!

[Offstage a door slams. Dad enters.]

DAD: *[exasperated]* Doesn't anybody have the Christmas spirit anymore? *[removes jacket, throws on chair]*

MOM: Apparently not. What has happened to this family today? Christy is upset, Blake had a bad experience with a friend, and now you. *[turns to DAD]* Will at least one of you tell me what's going on?

CHRISTY: *[enters]* I will.

[DAD, MOM, and BLAKE turn to CHRISTY.]

An Unexpected Christmas

MOM: Finally!

CHRISTY: Today after school my friend, Addison, and I went to a sale at the mall to see if we could find some of the gifts we want to give to our boyfriends. Addison saw this cool looking shirt for Rob and . . . *[hesitates]*

DAD: And?

CHRISTY: She carries this huge handbag *[spreads hands]* and she stuffed the shirt inside when nobody was looking! She acted like it was no big deal.

MOM: What did you say to her?

CHRISTY: We went to the ladies' room and I freaked out on her. I told her to put it back.

DAD: And?

CHRISTY: I said it was Christmas and didn't that mean anything to her? She laughed and said something about Christmas being the world's biggest sale. I was so annoyed!

MOM: Poor girl.

CHRISTY: And then she said I should lighten up and try a prank or two myself! I could hardly talk to her on the way home. She hasn't got a clue.

BLAKE: Sounds like Devin.

CHRISTY: I thought he was your best friend.

BLAKE: He is and that's what makes it so hard. He told me he thinks angels and big shiny stars in the sky are stupid. He's only in our Christmas play because his mom is making him do it.

MOM: But you told me you didn't want to be in the play either.

BLAKE: I don't want to be a shepherd again. I wanted to be Joseph but the only other boy besides me and Devin gets to do it. He's older.

MOM: *[looks at DAD]* So what happened to you?

DAD: I'm going to have to work late on Christmas Eve—very late. We have a big contract due right after the holiday and the boss is in a panic. I'll probably miss the church service.

MOM: He's just telling you now, two days before Christmas?

DAD: The client keeps changing the specs . . . it's complicated.

BLAKE: Wow, it's bad news all over the place.

MOM: *[shoos them towards chairs]* Sit down—all of you.

[BLAKE, CHRISTY, and DAD all sit, looking glum.]

MOM: *[picks up Bible]* You know, Christians have the most wonderful guide book in the world, written by Someone who loves us and only wants the very best for our lives. *[thumbs through Bible]* Here Blake, read this.

BLAKE: *[reads 1 Timothy 1:15]* Oh, Mom, this is . . .

MOM: *[interrupts]* Hold on, give me that *[takes Bible, turns to another verse]* Christy, you read this.

CHRISTY: *[reads 1 Corinthians 13:4-7]* Boy, I wish Addison would read this!

MOM: Shhh. *[motions to CHRISTY for Bible, flips to another verse]* And for you, read this. *[gives Bible to DAD]*

DAD: *[reads Romans 8:28]* I sure would love this to be true right now.

CHRISTY: I know why you chose that verse for Blake. He could set an example for Devin.

BLAKE: Easy for you to say.

CHRISTY: If he's forced to be in the Christmas play, why not try to make it fun for him? He probably just says those things because he's bored or angry.

BLAKE: I guess I could tell some jokes while we're practicing.

CHRISTY: *[laughs]* That would do it for me. Why did you give me the verse about love, Mom?

MOM: It's hardest to love someone when they're doing things that you know are wrong. Addison needs your friendship in a way you might not be able to understand right now.

[CAROLERS enter down center aisle quietly singing It Came Upon a Midnight Clear.]

BLAKE: What's that?

DAD: Sounds like carolers to me.

CHRISTY: Cool.

MOM: My goodness, we haven't had carolers in years!

DAD: I brought home a big tray of leftover cookies from our office party today.

MOM: I think we have some apple cider too.

DAD: Let's go out and listen.

[MOM, CHRISTY, BLAKE, and DAD step forward on the stage as CAROLERS approach.]

CHRISTY: *[looks intently at CAROLERS]* Oh, no!

BLAKE: What?

CHRISTY: I can't believe it! Addison is singing! And Rob too.

BLAKE: Maybe they'll sing *Grandma Got Run Over by a Reindeer!*

MOM: Blake, hush.

CHRISTY: *[in disgust]* What a hypocrite! I'm not going to listen to any songs they sing!

DAD: They're coming to the door. *[opens door]*

[ROB and ADDISON step away from the other CAROLERS and approach the family.]

An Unexpected Christmas

Dad: Nice job!

Rob: Thank you, Mr. Collins. We're bringing some of the sounds of the season to the neighborhood and . . . oh, hi Christy.

Addison: *[quickly]* We need to talk with Christy, Mr. Collins. Would that be okay?

Dad: Sure. *[motions to* Carolers*]* The rest of you may come in for cookies and cider.

*[*Carolers *laugh and nod as they move onstage and follow* Dad *offstage to kitchen.]*

Blake: Well, this should be interesting.

Addison: Hi, Blake.

Christy: *[pleadingly]* Mom!

Mom: *[guides* Blake *to kitchen offstage]* Come on, Blake, we have guests.

Addison: I have something to tell you, Christy.

Christy: *[arms across chest]* My little brother was right, this should be interesting.

Rob: Addison told me about the shirt.

Christy: *[astonished]* What?

Addison: I hope you're still willing to be my friend, Christy. All the way home this afternoon I thought about how angry you were and it began to eat at me what I'd done. So I told the truth and we took the shirt back.

Christy: Really?

Rob: *[laughs]* She told me all about it, Christy, and we drove back to the store. She told the manager what she did, and asked if she could pay for the shirt. *[pats chest]* Looks pretty good, huh?

Christy: Wow! *[hugs* Addison*]*

Addison: How could I sing carols about Christmas and have that on my conscience?

Rob: So here we are, singing up a storm and one of us is really thirsty!

Dad: *[enters holding cell phone up]* Wow.

Christy: You have a wow too, Dad?

Mom: *[enters]* I never saw such thirsty singers! *[looks at* Addison *and* Rob*]* You two better get in there.

*[*Addison *and* Rob *exit towards kitchen.]*

Dad: I just got a call from my boss. The client wants more changes and they agreed to postpone the project until the first week of January. So I'm all yours for Christmas!

Mom: Romans 8:28 at your service! *[hugs* Dad*]* Christmas Eve wouldn't be the same without you.

Blake: *[rushes in]* Wow!

[Mom, Dad, and Christy laugh.]

Blake: What?
Christy: Oh, we just know you have something good to tell us.
Blake: Why did the snowman cross the road?
Christy: This must be for Devin.
Mom: Why?
Blake: He didn't, Silly, a snowman can't walk.

[Mom, Dad, and Christy groan.]

Blake: Okay, I'll keep working on it.
Dad: Devin will probably love it, Blake.
Christy: Boy, this day sure had some unexpected turns in it!
Mom: Almost like someone knew our hearts and answered each of our needs.
Christy: What about you, Mom? What did you need?
Mom: Christy, you're right about how this day turned out. Mostly I needed my family to realize that where our Lord is concerned, we can always expect the unexpected.
Christy: You're right about that!

[Carolers enter laughing.]

Blake: Even these guys were unexpected!
Rob: Anyone want to join us? We have a few more houses to visit.
Dad: We're ready when you are!
Mom: That would be a lot of fun, but I have something I'd like to read first.
    [picks Bible up and reads Luke 2:1-14]
Christy: *[thoughtfully]* The real reason for the season.
Addison: I wish more people would stick up for the real Christmas like you do, Christy.
Christy: *[smiles at everyone]* Well, this group seems to be doing it!
Blake: I can't wait to sing with you guys!
Rob: How about *Grandma Got Run Over by a Reindeer*?
Blake: *[eyes open wide]* Really? Cool!
Rob: Just kidding, Blake. But maybe the congregation would like to join us.
    [indicates audience] We're singing *Joy to the World,* everyone.

[Congregation joins in as Carolers and family walk down center aisle singing.]

An Unexpected Christmas

Stranded

DIANA C. DERRINGER

Summary: A family, stranded by a snowstorm, moves from mutual irritation to appreciation for one another. They also gain a greater understanding of the first Christmas.

Characters:

MOM

DAD

TIM—teenage son

KARA—teenage daughter

Setting: a shabby and sparsely furnished motel room

Props: small desk with a lamp, telephone, and old telephone book; one straight chair at desk; twin size bed with worn bedspread; two cell phones; winter coats for everyone

Running Time: 8 minutes

All the family gathers in the motel room, brushing off imaginary snow and removing their coats. The teens slump on the floor against the side of the bed, arms crossed. Both scowl at their parents. MOM falls into the chair, and DAD stands near her.

MOM: *[in a positive tone]* Whew! Am I thankful we finally found a warm place to stay!

DAD: You're not the only one! I was beginning to think we'd be stuck in the car and either freeze to death or die of carbon monoxide poisoning trying to stay warm. I've seen weather like this on TV, but today's the first time I've experienced it . . . and I hope it's the last! *[look up]* Thank You, Lord!

TIM: *[sarcastically]* Right! We're just about the luckiest people I know. Stuck out here in the middle of nowhere with nothing to do for who knows how long, and Christmas is less than a week away!

KARA: *[mirroring TIM's sarcasm]* Yeah, whose bright idea was this, anyway? Why couldn't we just stay home like always and visit Uncle Walt after Christmas—like maybe next June?

MOM: Watch your mouths, both of you! *[to KARA]* You know as well as the rest of us that Uncle Walt probably won't make it through the holidays. So, if we want to see him, it's now or never.

KARA: *[half-heartedly]* Sorry, alright? I just can't figure out why we had to head out in the middle of a snow storm to see him.

DAD: If you recall, we had sunshine and fair weather when we left home. How were we supposed to know the worst blizzard of our lifetime was about to hit?

KARA: Duh! Weather forecasts!

MOM: One more smart remark like that, young lady, and you can forget . . .

KARA: *[holding up hands]* Alright, alright, I just hate being stuck here with nothing to do when all my friends are going to be together. Now I'll not only miss the ski trip, but we'll be lucky if we make it home for Christmas at all.

TIM: *[take cell phone from pocket]* At least we can keep up with what we're missing. *[begin texting and then look up, confused]* Or maybe not. *[shake phone]*

KARA: What? You've gotta be kidding! *[quickly pull phone from a pocket, punch in a number, and listen]* I can't believe this! *[jam phone back into pocket and head for the motel phone. After picking up the receiver, look at everyone in disbelief.]* This is unreal! Are we in some horrible second rate movie? There's no phone service!

MOM: At least we have heat.

TIM: Yeah, but what are we gonna eat? Pages from that yummy looking phone book from the dark ages?

DAD: Well, I did pack a few snacks.

TIM: *[sarcastically]* Great! Apples and granola bars I bet!

DAD: Well, sure. And I can't think of anything more filling and nutritious under the circumstances.

TIM: *[grudgingly]* I suppose they will keep us from starving to death.

DAD: Look, this isn't anybody's idea of a fun way to spend Christmas, but we're here, whether we like it or not. So why not make the best of it?

KARA: *[half sneering]* And just how do you propose we do that?

MOM: *[brightly]* Hey, remember when you two were little? If one of you said anything nasty to the other, you had to follow with two compliments?

TIM: I remember. I hated that game!

KARA: Yeah. *[punching brother's arm and laughing]* You never wanted to say anything nice to me, did you?

MOM: *[to TIM]* Well, buddy, get over it! The game is officially on the agenda again, and I believe each of us lags several compliments behind. So, Tim, you're first, and you can choose who receives your beginning words of kindness.

TIM: Lucky me! Let's see . . . Hmmm . . . *[look around at everyone]* Okay, shrimp, *[punching sister's arm]* you're not half bad most of the time.

MOM: That's not the most whole-hearted compliment I ever heard, but I guess it'll do for the moment. Who's next?

KARA: *[pushing brother's shoulder]* You're not so bad yourself. By the way, thanks for covering for me the other day when I didn't have time for chores.

TIM: No problem. *[smiling]* Just don't let it happen again.

KARA: And, hey dad, I'm sorry I gave you such a hard time about getting stuck. I know you didn't plan it, and you and mom take good care of us. Thanks for not warping us over the head for our big mouths.

DAD: You're welcome. Besides you're actually great kids most of the time, and we're proud to be your parents.

MOM: Yes, we are. We love you both so much, and even though we make mistakes, we do try our best.

TIM: Yeah, we know. I'm afraid I can't say I always try my best.

KARA: Me either.

TIM: But we love you too.

KARA: Hey, this is beginning to sound like one of those sappy TV shows . . . you know the kind the two of you *[looking at parents]* watch over and over and over?

MOM: *[beckoning motion with hands]* I like it. I like it. Keep those cards and letters coming!

TIM: Hey guys, maybe being stuck here won't be so bad. Can't think of anyone nicer to spend time with in a cramped stuffy room with a blizzard outside. Besides, the first Christmas family's circumstances weren't the best in the world either, right?

DAD: That's right. They didn't even have the benefit of a crummy little motel room to share with other grumpy travelers. *[with conviction]* But the circumstances of that night changed our world and *[gesturing toward the others]* each of our lives forever.

KARA: Merry Christmas, Mom and Dad.

MOM and DAD: Merry Christmas to you too.

TIM: *[standing with arms outstretched and imitating Tiny Tim from "A Christmas Carol"]* And God bless us everyone!

[All laugh as lights go out. A voice offstage reads Luke 2:1-20.]

Stranded

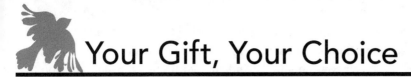

Your Gift, Your Choice

DIANA C. DERRINGER

Summary: A teenage girl tells about her grandmother's unique Christmas
   challenge.
Character:
Teenage Girl
Setting: any location
Props: contemporary teen clothing
Running Time: 5 minutes

*The Teenage Girl walks to center stage and speaks with enthusiasm and
animation.*

My grams . . . what can I say? *[raise hands and shrug shoulders]* She is *so*
amazing and *way* cool, *[pause]* considering her age and all, of course. She loves
me, no doubt about it. But don't think for a minute that she lets me get by with
much. And I have no idea how she learned to be so sneaky—a good sneaky, but
sneaky nonetheless!

Like the other day . . . she *[extend hand to the side]* hands me an envelope
and says it contains a little something extra for Christmas, and I can use it any
way I choose. She even offers to take me shopping, *[pause]* if I want to go. And
I'm like, well, yeah! When do we leave?

Then she says that she needs to make a couple of other stops on the way
if I don't mind. So I think, *[shrug]* okay, no problem. I can tag along for a few
minutes in order to hit the malls later.

So off we go! First stop, a class at her church is just completing an English
as a Second Language lesson. She introduced me to a couple of girls my age and
asked me to talk with them a few minutes. They needed to practice their speaking
skills. Although they had a little trouble, I could understand them okay. Then they
told me I was the first English speaking person their age who had talked with
them, and they kept thanking me and thanking me.

After a few minutes the teacher said they could all go to the clothes closet
next door to try on coats. Most of them came from warm countries and had no
winter clothes. *[in disgust]* Well, the only coats their size obviously had hard
lives and looked more like something other people's grandmas might wear . . .
[smiling] not mine, of course. *[bewildered]* But those girls thanked the teacher
like they'd received the greatest gift in the world.

[firmly] When we left I told Grams our new friends deserved better coats than that and someone should do something about it! Grams just nodded and said, *[quietly]* "Yes, someone should." "And another thing," I said, "why don't more girls their age spend time with them?" And Grams replied, "Why, indeed?"

Next we dropped in on a luncheon. A missionary speaker described her work in a country where almost no one had heard of Jesus or had a Bible. Afterwards I asked Grams if she had ever heard of such a thing. She nodded her head and said that same situation exists in many countries.

[indignantly] I told Grams that's not right. Everyone should hear about Jesus, so why don't church members do something? *[more calmly]* Grams said she totally agreed.

Grams volunteers at a local food pantry, so we made our last stop there. She asked the workers if they had enough for the rest of the week. Since they receive more requests this time of year, they said the food supply would be really close. *[exasperated]* I couldn't believe it! Here we live in a neighborhood with supermarkets and restaurants everywhere you look, and yet there are people who don't have enough to eat! What's wrong with this picture?

I asked Grams if that didn't make her want to quit and go home. She shook her head and asked me, "If I don't help, who will?"

"Well, we have a whole community of people with more food than they can possibly eat, and a lot of them should go on diets anyway," I said. Again my Grams agreed.

I'll admit I can be a little slow, but I started to get the picture! "Grams," I said, "what do you really want me to do with this Christmas money?"

Hugging me close, she answered, *[slowly, clearly, and with emphasis]* "Honey, that decision is up to you." *[long pause before exit]*

Your Gift, Your Choice

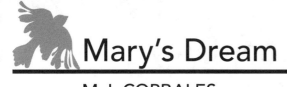

Mary's Dream

M.J. CORRALES

Joseph, I had a dream last night. I don't really understand it all, but I want to tell you about it. I think it was about our Son, about a birthday celebration for Him. The people had been anticipating it for many weeks. They had decorated their homes and gone shopping many times and had purchased elaborate gifts. It was very strange, though, because the presents were not for our Son. People had wrapped all the gifts in beautiful paper and tied them with lovely bows and placed them under trees.

Yes, that's right, trees. Right there inside their homes. They had decorated the trees also. The branches were full of glowing balls and sparkling ornaments. The tops of the trees had stars or figures on them. It was beautiful. Everyone was laughing and happy about the decorations and about the trees and the gifts.

But they were giving the gifts to each other, Joseph, not to our Son. I really don't think they knew who He was at all. His name was never mentioned. No one ever said anything about Him. Doesn't it seem odd for people to go to all that trouble for someone's birthday whom they don't even know? I even had the strangest feeling that if our Son had attended some of these celebrations, He would not have been welcome.

Everything was so beautiful, Joseph. But it made me want to cry. How sad for Jesus not to be wanted at His own birthday party. I am so glad it was only a dream. How terrible if it had been real.

The Shepherd Boy

M.J. CORRALES

I had gone out to tend the sheep that night with my older brothers. They don't often let me go along with them so I was really looking forward to it. But the night was still and all was quiet. I was getting a little sleepy and, well, bored. I remember wishing for something to happen so I could wake up.

Boy, did I get my wish! One minute all was still and quiet except for gentle sounds coming from the sheep—and then, the next minute! Wow! This bright light appeared right above us, shining through the night sky. Something inside of me said it was an angel. Since I had never seen an angel before, I don't know how I knew this—I just did.

The angel spoke to us and said a baby was being born over in Bethlehem that very night. The angel said the baby was the Savior, Christ the Lord!

Instantly the whole sky was lit up with a wondrous light and many more angels joined the first one! They were all praising God and saying, "Glory to God in the highest, and on earth peace, goodwill toward men!"

Then—as suddenly as they had appeared—they were gone! And the sky was once more dark and still. If any one of us had been alone, it would not have been difficult to convince ourselves we had but imagined it—the angels, the light, the praising—the good news of a baby being born in a stable.

But we were all together, and we had seen it all together. We stood there, looking at one another in astonishment, not knowing what we should do. Then my oldest brother said we should go down to the village to see this baby, this Savior, for ourselves. We all agreed, thinking perhaps we needed to see with our eyes what our minds could still not quite grasp.

Someone asked what about the flock and we all turned as one to look at the sheep. But they were all peaceful and quiet, as if the great light in the sky and the rejoicing of the angels had never occurred. We knew that God who sent the angels to us that night would also be able to watch over our sheep while we were away, seeking the baby.

A baby! A baby from God! The first angel had said we would find Him wrapped in swaddling clothes, lying in a manger. I wondered at the meaning of "swaddling" even as I ran to catch up with my brothers who were already making their way down the hill. What a strange word that was. I just hoped I would recognize it when I saw it.

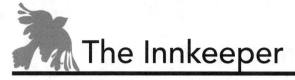

The Innkeeper

M.J. CORRALES

I've been innkeeper here for many years. My wife and I manage to make a fair living at it. Of course, we depend on the many celebrations and special occasions several times a year to really bring in the people from the countryside to crowd my inn. All those extra people—and their money!

That's why when I heard of Rome (I spit on Rome!) telling us to register for taxing—so they could get even more money from us—I thought we would really get some visitors then! Just between you and me, I even increased the price for lodging. Wasn't that clever of me? How would anybody know? You can't fault me for trying to get all I can for myself, can you? For taking advantage of a situation that Rome (I spit on Rome!) created? If I don't look out for me and mine, who will? No one else, that's for sure!

But let me tell you about that night. They looked like any other couple, tired and weary from the road. I told them I had no room in my inn and told them to go on their way. But my wife heard me and came out to see. She heard the man say his wife was about to have a baby and she desperately needed a place to rest. Well, that didn't mean anything to me; they were just another fare I didn't have room for. But my wife—she would give away everything we had if I didn't stop her! She told the man they could use our stable out back, if they didn't mind the smell.

I heard later that the woman had given birth to a son that night. All sorts of people went out there to see that couple and their newborn son. I supposed if I had known she really was going to have the baby then, I could maybe have found them a better place. I could have found them something inside. But I didn't know. How was I to know?

Can you imagine all that fuss over a baby anyway? Wonder what's so special about him?

The Birth of a Song!

CAROL S. REDD

Summary: Creating an awesome silence in which to completely absorb the miracle of the Savior's birth.

Characters:

NARRATOR

CHOIR, SOLOISTS, MUSICIANS

Setting: church auditorium decorated for Christmas

Set: dark, quiet setting with no lighting during opening and closing narratives. Narrator is located off-stage and out of sight. Lighting can be adjusted as needed during choir, soloists', and musicians' presentations.

Props: off-stage microphone

Costumes: choir dressed in normal choir robes or street clothes depending on type of music being presented

Running Time: 30–60 minutes (can be adjusted depending on songs chosen)

Auditorium should be completely dark as narrator begins reading from off-stage area.

NARRATOR: Quiet. Stillness. Silence. Something miraculous is about to happen. Something beyond description, beyond imagination, beyond words.

Come with us as we travel in mind, in heart, in spirit back to a place called Bethlehem, for a glorious birth—the birth of a song.

This song is for you. A song that will heal hearts thought beyond healing, comfort spirits who need to find peace, calm lives once filled with sorrow, and mend what this world has broken.

This song is for you. A song that gives hope when you feel life has no purpose, courage when you have none of your own, love when you feel undeserving, and reason when there's none to be found.

Our song is gentle, powerful, tender, and strong. Our song is called precious. Our song is called holy. Our song is called Jesus.

The Birth of a Song!

[Soft lighting gradually comes up as the choir, soloists, and musicians present the Christmas story in song.]

[Lighting gradually goes down until auditorium is completely dark as narrator begins reading from off-stage area.]

NARRATOR: We have witnessed the birth—the birth of a song. Our song! The song of all those who follow Jesus!

It is the song that makes possible the impossible, gives hope in hopelessness, provides joy in joylessness, and offers grace when none is deserved.

Our song is called precious. Our song is called holy. Our song is called Jesus. Our song is forever!

The Birth of a Song!

What if There Were No Christmas?

VANESSA BUSH

[cue somber music]

What if there were no Christmas?

No "Silent Night," no twinkle lights, no *It's a Wonderful Life.*
No angels singing, no jingle bells ringing.
No boxes and bows, no swaddling clothes, no Jack Frost nipping at your nose.
No cattle lowing or candles glowing.
No Mary, meek and mild. No holy, perfect child.
No tidings of great joy, no little drummer boy.
No star in the east, no greatest-become-least, no eternal high priest.

What if a Savior had never come to Earth?
What if there hadn't ever been a virgin birth?

What if it were just us with no one to fall back on but our own fault-ridden
    selves?
What if a living illustration of peace and love and hope had never been born?
What if *that* baby had been just like every other baby?
What if our God had refused to humble Himself and live as one of His own
    creation?
What if we were responsible for our own holiness?

What if there were no peace?
What if there were no light?
What if there were no hope?

[end somber music]

[cue hopeful music]

But Christmas *did* come!

Our Savior didn't arrive as a warrior king
but He came as an unassuming infant.
Our Wonderful, Counselor was born in an obscure village.
The Mighty God lay in a manger.
The Everlasting Father had a teenage mother and a working-class stepfather.
The Prince of Peace slept near livestock.
The Word Made Flesh walked on dusty roads.
The Great I Am wore a crown of thorns.
The Light of the World endured a cross.

He was born to die to cover our wrongs.
He became a servant so that we would have a chance for peace, for hope, for life.

What If There Were No Christmas?

A Promise Fulfilled

DIANA C. DERRINGER

Summary: A widow briefly details her life and encounter with the promised Messiah.
Character: ANNA, THE PROPHETESS
Setting: the temple in Jerusalem
Props: columns or a picture of temple columns in the background
Running Time: 2 minutes

When ANNA reaches center stage she extends her hands, rubs and inspects the top of them, shakes her head slightly, and begins talking slowly.

Eighty-four years old. How hard to believe I've lived eighty-four years. Why it seems only yesterday I was a little girl in my father's home.

My role as a prophetess surprised no one, since I come from a family devoted to God. *[pause]* My husband, as fine a man as I've ever known, also followed the ways of the Lord. *[look into distance]* But he died so young. *[sigh]* Our seven years together flew by, and it gets harder and harder to remember how he looked. *[shake head]* Oh well, I mustn't dwell on the past.

As a widow, I decided to make this temple *[sweeping hand motion]* my home. Worshipping, fasting, and praying filled my days and nights. Although not a route many choose, it's provided a satisfying life, and I have no complaints. Like many, my hope focused on the promised coming of our Savior. Well aware my time on Earth grew short, I continued to wait and pray.

God's Spirit revealed to Simeon, an older man from this area, that he would live to see the Savior. Today I saw him talking with a couple in the temple. He held a baby no more than a few days old. I assumed the family came to dedicate their child to the Lord, as expected of all new parents. Simeon's face radiated such joy as he praised God. When I came near, I heard him bless them and tell the woman of her child's future. The longer he talked, the more obvious his words became, *[emphatically]* and I knew! I knew this baby was our promised Messiah!

[Hold hands up.] Oh, how I glorify God. *[Bring hands down.]* I did see Him, and now I must tell others! *[walking toward exit]* I must tell them He's come!

Follow with a song proclaiming Jesus' coming, such as "Joy to the World" or "Go Tell It on the Mountain."

A Promise Fulfilled

A Mother's Heart

KAREN M. LEET

Oh, my wonderful and amazing God! Just see what You have done! Here in my arms. Here is the baby, my own sweet precious boy. Like any other baby—I've seen so many, held so many, watched and helped at the bedside of new mothers. And here I am, new mother with a baby of my own. Warm, close held in my arms, against my body—part of me—and, oh my God, part of You.

Holding Him, my sweet little baby boy, I can scarce believe it—how You chose me, called me, gave me this promise, this incredible moment.

And here He is, so real. So small to hold all wrapped and bundled up against night chill. Fresh hay around us. A warm, safe place. A quiet time together with my Joseph here beside us. I see in my Joseph's eyes the wonder of it all.

Yet, I can hardly believe it—who this babe is, how He has come to be and the future You have for Him. I push those thoughts away. Not yet. Not now. For now I hold my baby, my sweet boy child, and He sleeps.

I check him carefully, as every new mother does. Count His toes and fingers. Touch the soft fuzz of hair on His head, and marvel that this child was hidden inside me such a short time ago.

Part of me yearns for this to be an ordinary birth, an ordinary time, private and quiet, no one else's business, except Joseph and me.

And for just these few moments it seems to be—our time, alone together with the baby, this beloved child. Our eyes meet, Joseph's and mine. He leans in close, my Joseph, to watch over us, and I see in his eyes how much he loves us. He will never allow harm to touch us.

Thank You, God, for Joseph.

You have chosen well in him. A fine and decent man. A good and godly man. A true and honest man. Thank You, God.

Joseph smiles at me and touches the babe, gently, as if half afraid. Our eyes lock over the baby's head. No words between us, but we know this moment, this quiet moment together, cannot last.

I know in my heart they will come soon. The others, the ones who will know who He is, this child of mine. For this one moment, though, I am bathed in love and silence, safety and peace, and that is enough.

I hear them coming now. Eager, rushing footsteps. The first of many, they're coming to see my baby—God's Baby—the Promised One, the Holy One, the One sent to be King of all kings.

I take a deep breath and hear Joseph sigh beside me as we prepare for them to come. Oh, Lord, God almighty, give us the strength we will need for all that lies ahead of us, amen and amen.

And now they come—for the Child, the Son of almighty God, our precious little one, our Jesus.

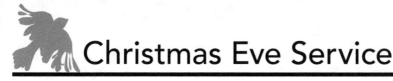

Christmas Eve Service

STACY A. POPEJOY

Over the years, the *facts* of Christmas have become co-mingled with the *fictions* of Christmas to the point where many people no longer recognize what the holiday truly represents. Christmas is a warm, wonderful holiday, with many joyous sentiments and traditions. It is, and should be, a time of great celebration, but we must recognize what it really is, and why we celebrate. We must remember the words of the angel to the shepherds, "A Savior has been born to you. He is Christ the Lord."

[Congregation sings, "I Heard the Bells On Christmas Day."]

1. Promise to the Hopeless

Dark. Helpless. Hopeless. That is the only way to truly describe the world that day. God, the creator and sustainer of all people, had been silent for too long. He had hidden His shining glory from His people, leaving them exposed to, and under the control of an unfeeling, unrelenting Roman government. By this time, God's people had not known true peace for centuries. They experienced only periodic, short-lived, moments of happiness in their lives when and if the heavy hand of Roman rule might loosen its grip of bondage and power, thus teasing Israel with a slight, blurry glimpse of hope. But these gestures were consistently empty, as there was never an intent to bring freedom or peace; only more and increased pain, as Rome was a kingdom which thrived upon hatred, jealousy, pride, and political ambition. For God's people—enslaved, battered, and helpless—any hope for peace or freedom had been long since buried in the past.

But God's people were given the promise of the prophet, "Out of [Bethlehem] will come a ruler over Israel. He will stand and shepherd his flock in the strength of the Lord and they will live securely and He will be their peace." What wonderful news this must have been to ears that had been deafened for so long. The Savior, the true ruler of the world, had come and through Him, hope and peace and freedom were brought to all who recognized Him. His was to be a power that would overcome and conquer the mightiest of earthly rulers, and His was to be a kingdom that would bring peace forever!

[Congregation sings, "O Come, O Come Emmanuel" and "O Little Town of Bethlehem."]

[Light candles in Section 1.]

2. Proclamation to the Shepherds

"I bring you good news of great joy." These were the words of the angel to the shepherds on that quiet night. This message was intended to bring joy, and joy it did bring. God had presented the world with a wonderful gift. The long awaited, promised, Savior: a Shepherd to guide His people and a King who would represent them. All that the people had needed, prayed for, and waited for had finally come to them. For these people who had for so long been living without peace, light, hope, and life, God's promise of all that and more was now being offered to them through the message of the angels. What good news that was! This gift of love—God Himself, clothed as an infant—had finally come to be right here with them, in the flesh. Immanuel. Jesus. The very definition of great joy! Thus, the first Christmas celebration was about to begin!

[Congregation sings, "The First Noel" and "Hark The Herald Angels Sing."]

[Light candles in Section 2.]

3. Presentation to the Shepherds

The shepherds made no plans for an elaborate party. No special notices of their pilgrimage were sent out. They didn't bother with fancy clothes or to prepare a royal feast. They just went. They hurried off to see these things that were told to them. They went to give honor to the one who was born to bring joy back to their empty hearts. They went to offer those hearts to Him, the Son of God, their Savior, as an act of worship and celebration.

As well, wise men from the East traveled to that place to see Him who was born to bring joy into the world. These men, though rich, happy, and fulfilled by the world's standards, came to honor and worship Him because they believed that the true King, the true fulfillment, and true source of joy, was given by God in the form of that little boy. Though they came bearing costly gifts to *give*, they came knowing they would truly *receive* that which is priceless. Oh, what great joy!

[Congregation sings, "Angels We Have Heard On High" and "Angels From the Realms of Glory."]

[Light candles in Section 3.]

[Congregation sings, "O Come Let Us Adore Him."]

Christmas is the celebration of God's greatest gift—life. The angel told the shepherds that it was good news of great joy that would be for all people. What was this good news? A Savior was born to them. God looked upon all humans, saw us in our need, and responded with the most practical gift ever given. When informing Joseph of Mary's pregnancy and God's plan, the angel said to him, "You are to give Him the name Jesus, because He will save His people from their sins". His people's sins. Every person's sin. Every one of us was lost, hopeless, and dying in our sin. There was no way out. All of our efforts to bring about forgiveness and reconciliation were useless. Sin was going to destroy us. All of us. But God said, "No." His love would not let it happen. So He put into action His plan for reconciliation. He sent us His one and only Son, who Himself would know no sin, to take *our* sin, to forgive *our* sin, and to receive the punishment for *our* sin, in *our* place. God, by His own requirement, sentenced His own perfect Son to death, so that we—the unworthy, the broken, and the sinful could have the gift of life. What else could any one ask for? What more practical gift could any one ever get? What better reason could every one have to celebrate? "The punishment that brought us peace was upon Him, and by His wounds we are healed."

*[Congregation sings,
"O Come Let Us Adore
Him."]*

4. Peace to the World

That night, in a small town in Judea, a child was born. Quietly and unannounced to all but a few shepherds, He made His entrance into the world. Though small in the eyes of the world and helpless in the minds of people, He was God's answer to the centuries old petitions of His people; the all but forgotten source of hope and peace. By those words of the angel, "A Savior has been born to you; He is Christ the Lord," all who live in this dark world today have this same hope. Jesus, born so many years ago, was born for us as well. It is still His desire to bring peace to all people, and to reign as their King.

Each year at Christmas, people send themselves into financial, emotional, and physical depression trying to bring into their lives and the lives of others the feeling of joy and peace that Christmas promises. But the joy and peace of Christmas is *not a feeling*. It cannot be purchased, created, decorated, or wrapped. There is no program or accomplishment that will activate it in a person's heart. The joy and peace of Christmas is embodied in the child Himself. Jesus Christ, God's free gift, is the great joy promised by the angel. Only by seeking Him and sharing Him with others will each man, woman, and child find the true peace and joy of Christmas.

As we celebrate Christmas, let us not neglect to recognize the *truth* about Christmas. Yes, it is about peace on Earth, but the celebration is about the birth of a King who brought peace—to Earth, to our hearts, to our very lives—for all eternity!

[Congregation sings, "O Holy Night," and "Joy to the World."]

[Light candles in Section 4.]

[Congregation sings, "O Come All Ye Faithful."]

Poems

The Silent Night
Dianne McIntosh

Silent night,
I can't hear a thing
except the deafening ring
of the love of God.

Holy night,
when the veil is torn
and the Word of God
takes on human form.

All is calm
for those who've read the signs
and waited patiently
through the years of time.

All is bright
as the angels sing
in the star filled sky
to announce the King.

Follow the Star
Crystal Bowman

Follow the star to the manger,
for a newborn baby is born.
Follow the star to the manger,
He sleeps all cozy and warm.

Follow the star to the manger,
to worship the newborn King.
Follow the star to the manger,
to offer your praises and sing.

Come bring your gifts to Jesus,
bring your treasure from afar.
This way to baby Jesus—
follow the shining star.

Come now and worship the Savior,
God's Son who was born Christmas night.
He is our Lord and Messiah,
so follow the heavenly light.

Follow the star to the manger.
The star will show you the way.
Believe in Jesus your Savior
and give Him your heart today.

Where Can We Find Jesus?
Crystal Bowman

The angels told the shepherds,
"Our Savior's been born today.
You'll find Him in a manger
upon a bed of hay."

The shepherds quickly ran to town
and found the baby there.
Then they went out rejoicing—
they had good news to share!

People came to worship Him,
they came from near and far.
The wise men found the Savior too
by following a star.

So where can we find Jesus
as Christmas day draws near?
Is Jesus in the busyness
of all our Christmas cheer?

Is Jesus in the presents
that we place beneath the tree?
Do we speak of Him at mealtime
with our friends and family?

Do we share God's love and kindness
with those who have a need?
Are we quick to help our neighbor
or do a thoughtful deed?

If that's the way we live our lives
then others just might see
that Jesus is alive today—
He lives in you and me.

The Message
Karen M. Leet

Angels poured down from the sky
with wondrous news from God on high—
a Child is born this Christmas Day,
come to take our sins away,
come to save us all from grief,
come to bring us sweet relief,
come to bring us hope and joy,
come for us this precious boy.

Angels sang and praised His name
on the night that Jesus came,
Child of goodness, Child of grace,
come for everyone in this place,
come for every adult and child,
precious Jesus meek and mild.

Angels came to spread the story
of Jesus come to give God glory,
of Jesus in a cattle stall,
Lamb of God sent for us all,
of Jesus bedded in the hay,
sent to us this Christmas day.

Angels poured down from the sky
with their message from God on high.

Child
Karen M. Leet

Child of mercy, child of grace—
You are welcome in this place.
Gentle Savior, meek and mild,
Lamb of God, Christmas child,
come and fill our hearts with joy,
precious Jesus, God's own boy.

God's only Son, with radiant face,
we come to worship You in this place.
We come to offer You all our love,
Prince of Peace sent from above.
Child of mercy, child of grace—
thank You for coming to this place.

Then Christmas Comes
Susan Sundwall

The hurry and bustle are over.
The cooking and baking are done.
Chilly winds blow down the chimney
and children are eager for fun.

The pageant practice is finished.
The choir has mastered each song.
Our hearts burst full with the season;
we listen as church bells are rung.

Slowly, like soft falling snowflakes
a calmness creeps over the earth.
Then Christmas comes close to embrace us
with joy at the news of His birth.

Come Now You Joyous
Susan Sundwall

Come now you joyous,
come to the stall
in Bethlehem's manger
where God welcomes all.

Kneel down in wonder
at what you see there,
the child sent to save you
from sin's crippling snare.

Come now you joyous
and tell of His birth
as angel songs echo
Heaven's anthem on Earth.

My Greatest Gift
Diana C. Derringer

Our Christmas lists are often long.
The tasks and wants go on and on.
We rush from work to home to store,
and to events with food galore.

We buy and wrap and buy some more
while bills pile high and debits soar.
We craft and sing and greet and bake,
compete with neighbors who decorate.

Then when it's over we breathe a sigh
and ask ourselves again just why
we wear ourselves into the ground
forgetting what is most profound.

God gave Himself, His greatest gift,
because our world was set adrift
by sins and wrongs within each life
that led to sorrow, pain, and strife.

Let's focus on just why He came,
He loved enough to take our blame.
God gave His best with no regrets.
Can we, His children, offer less?

A Shepherd Came
Charlotte Adelsperger

Angels called to shepherds in fields!
I so love this awesome story.
Shepherds rushed to the Christ child,
heavens radiating God's glory!

Today Christ calls to me in life
and gives transforming power.
I know him as my Savior—
shepherd of my soul each hour.

Glory to God
Lorena E. Worlein

"Glory to God in the highest"
the angels in chorus did sing,
proclaiming the joyous glad tidings,
announcing the birth of a King.

The shepherds of Bethlehem heard them
early that first Christmas morn,
bringing good news to all people,
Jesus, our Savior is born.

The wise men kept searching the heavens.
They looked for a glorious star.
And when, at long last, they beheld it,
they journeyed and traveled afar.

The shepherds and wise men adored Him—
the babe who was born on that night.
They knelt down and worshipped before Him.
They felt a great joy at the sight.

O, come join the wise men and shepherds
and sing with the angels above,
"Glory to God in the highest."
Give Him your worship and love.

Best Gift of All
Douglas Raymond Rose

While some spend tons of money
shopping the Christmas malls,
God gave to us His holy Son
the best Christmas gift of all.

What God gave the world is priceless.
Our sweet Savior gave His all.
God gave His gift of salvation,
the best Christmas gift of all.

The Shepherd's Story
Lorena E. Worlein

The sheep seemed restless on that night,
and I felt restless too.
I don't know why I felt that way.
I really had no clue.
I stood there gazing at the sky.
The stars were shining bright.
One seemed to have a special glow
and gave a radiant light.

When suddenly before my eyes
an angel did appear.
I was astonished at the sight.
My heart was filled with fear.
The angel said, "Fear not! I bring
good news to those on Earth.
This night is born in Bethlehem
a child of royal birth.

His name shall be called Christ the Lord
a Savior, sent to men
who sit in darkness, without light,
to give them hope again."
And then I saw a heavenly host
proclaiming from the sky
God's message to a weary world
"Glory to God on high."

A Christmas Cradle
Douglas Raymond Rose

Come to the Christmas cradle.
Come see Immanuel so dear.
The Christ child who dwells among us
is the Savior born calmly here.

Mary and Joseph hover around Him.
His name is known to each boy and girl.
Born a small child, yet He is a King,
the sovereign Savior of the world.